M000266819

HOUSE EQUANIMITY / JOSEPH N. BIONDO

A CONCRETE CUBE MELD

MASTERPIECE
SERIES

HOUSE EQUANIMITY / JOSEPH N. BIONDO

FOREWORD BY **WENDY ORNELAS** | INTRODUCTION BY **BYRON HAWES** | EPILOGUE BY **JOSEPH N. BIONDO**
COMPLETED BUILDING PHOTOGRAPHY BY **STEVE WOLFE**

OSCAR RIERA OJEDA
PUBLISHERS

CONTENTS

FOREWORD
BY WENDY ORNELAS

e·qua·nim·i·ty, *n.* mental or emotional stability or composure, esp. under tension or strain; calmness; equilibrium.[1]

I first met Joe Biondo while he was a visiting professor at Kansas State University. As a practicing architect and professor at the university, I was immediately impressed with Joe's fanatic attention to craftsmanship and materiality. It was a breath of fresh air to have him teach this critical perspective to our students. Nearly two decades later, I still see the impact he made on his previous students, who will often ask about him and speak fondly of the rigor and attention to detail they learned through his design studio. Their semester with Joe made a significant impression on their lasting view of the profession.

House Equanimity clearly reflects the importance of an architecture of the senses – sight, smell, sound, taste, touch and movement. It is a place | space of rigor, with an attention to detail, materiality, making, craftsmanship, and the importance of tactility. All of these ideals are one's he impressed upon his students.

> *Critical Regionalism seeks to complement our normative visual experience by readdressing the tactile range of human perceptions. . . Its capacity to arouse the impulse to touch returns the architect to the poetics of construction and to the erection of works in which the tectonic value of each component depends upon the density of its objecthood.*[2]

This house reveals a passion for making a place that is built out of, and inspired by, the region. It is not only about the poetic, but also of its position. The tactility of the materials, and the process of the construction reveal themselves in the art of the place.

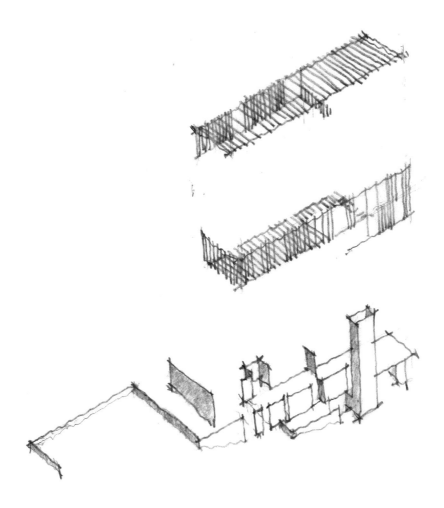

House Equanimity grew out of a connection to the senses. Its design is an unconscious reflection of the body in its scale and proportions. The slowness and layers of thought embedded in the design process of the house allowed Joe time to reveal a deep connection to the visual, sound, touch and movement within the space. The nature of making and the use of natural materials created an expression of the history and age of the house. The design was less about image than it was about freezing a moment in time through construction and allowing the project to speak of its materiality and of its age. The slowness of making became an experiential quality revealed through the body, movement and the senses.

In an era of global architecture the work of Joe Biondo continues to reflect the significance of place. All of our senses are heightened when we are in spaces he has designed. One reads his focus and passion. These are essential qualities of the profession I continue to teach my students.

Wendy Ornelas, FAIA
Professor, APDesign, Kansas State University
Manhattan, Kansas

[1]*The Random House Dictionary of the English Language.* Second edition. Unabridged. New York: Random House. 1987.
[2]Frampton, Kenneth. *Towards a Critical Regionalism: Six Points for an Architecture of Resistance.* 1983. In Foster, Hal (editor) Postmodern Culture. London: Pluto Press. Page 29.

INTRODUCTION
BY BYRON HAWES

HOUSE EQUANIMITY
NORTHAMPTON, PENNSYLVANIA, USA

'Perhaps we will cling longest to the symbol of "house" as we have known it, or perhaps we will realize that in accommodating ourselves to a new world the most important step in avoiding retrogression into the old, is a willingness to understand and to accept contemporary ideas in the creation of an environment that is responsible for shaping the largest part of our living and thinking.'

So wrote John Entenza in Arts & Architecture Magazine's seminal 1945 announcement of their iconoclastic Case Study Houses programme.

Typically noted primarily for its mandate of designing and building efficient and inexpensive model homes for a post-WWII society, the programme's broader philosophical implications, particularly in the furtherance of Corbusian modernist tenets and investigations into the shifting quotidian and spatial dynamics sought by contemporary lifestyles, have played a much larger role in our evolving understanding of the 'home'.

As we now embody it, the home must be as much free-form studio as isolationist private dwelling. It must accommodate the programmatic instincts of the owner's lifestyle rather than the other way around; be interpretive of, rather than imposing upon, their chosen way of living. Provide comfort and solace for its inhabitants; allowing them the time and space to be free. A machine for living, yes, but also a machine for being.

Residential Philosophy
Joseph Biondo's House Equanimity intuitively understands this. A mature, elegant, considered work of great beauty; this is a house borne of possibility. A whispering soliloquy in the face of many of his contemporaries more raucous monologues.

Nestled into the sloping topography of its site, on an unassuming and unremarkable eastern Pennsylvanian subdivision, Biondo's house represents a specific understanding of modern residential architecture, encompassing the environmental, the aesthetic, and the functional.

BYRON HAWES is a New York-based writer and designer. He is the founder of the underground design magazine The Après Garde, and a co-founder of I-V, a boutique architecture and design firm that has done projects including a recording studio for OVOsound, Campari's Canadian HQ, and Spin Toronto. He is contributing editor: architecture and design at Hypebeast, and previously served as a consulting editor at Architectural Digest China, as well as contributing to publications including Monocle, Wallpaper, Apartamento, and Azure, amongst others.

He has also authored or co-authored the books 'We Are Wonderful: 25 Years of Design and Fashion in Limburg', 'The Landscape Architecture of Paul Sangha', 'Bedmar & Shi: In The Tropics', 'Post-Industrial Brutalism and the Daiquiri', and several titles in ORO's Masterpiece Series.

An orthogonal plan, essentially a group of stacked cubes writ-rectangular, is, at certain angles, reminiscent of the Eames House in the Palisades, at others of a Dessau-era Bauhaus submarine. Its contours are intrinsically modernist in bent, echoing much of the minimalist, clean line thinking so beloved of Walter Gropius and the Bauhauslers, which were ultimately catalyzed throughout America due to the famed 'International Style' MoMA exhibition, curated by Philip Johnson and Henry-Russell Hitchcock. While not germanely 'of' the stylistic impetuses of either the European or Californian modernists, House Equanimity echoes many of their aesthetic advantages; espousing order, balance, and symmetry, while retaining a feeling of life and warmth, that many early modernists eschewed in their quest for philosophical casting off of bourgeois tropes.

From a geometric perspective, as well as in its interpretation of optimal house size, it evokes California modernism; not specifically the Case Study houses, but, more broadly, the desert modernist tracts developed by the Alexanders in Palm Springs, and

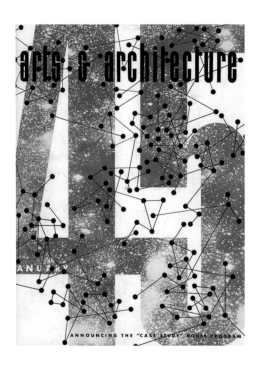

Charles and Ray Eames House, Los Angeles, Caifornia, 1949.

designed by the likes of William Krisel and Donald Wexler. Modest footprints, shared bathroom(s), and a strong focus placed on the juxtaposition between indoor-outdoor space. A collectivist approach to the typical delineation between nature and enclosure.

The house further distinguishes itself in that it actively interacts with a theoretically lesser building site, that which is sloping, and turns that supposed disadvantage into a positive force, using the topographical curvature as natural shielding to create privacy. The house is nestled directly into its landscape, rather than taking the typical architectural perspective, which is to find a flat, unencumbered plot of land so that the building itself can be the focus. This is used to particular advantage on the sprawling open terrace to the house's southwest. By shielding the southern elevation through clever reading of the east-west downward sloping site, the terrace is naturally accorded increased privacy simply through an informed reading of the site's inherent topography. To sit outside on this terrace is to feel at ease; protected though not isolated, as no large scale wall is necessary to separate the outdoor spatial experience from the street.

The ground floor echoes Corbusier's preference for the internal open plan and the free façade bolstered with horizontal windows. Kitchen, dining room, and double-height living room are unconstricted, naturally progressing from 'room' to 'room' through perceived separations identified by furniture placement rather than structural impediments or implications. See, for example, an ensconced concrete fireplace so minimalistically beautiful that the term 'living room' seems woefully inadequate, bringing to mind instead evocations of the picturesque snow-laden rural

idylls of Hemingway's Austrian trips in 'There is Never any End to Paris'. Tropical vernacular architecture typically takes great pains to highlight mixed-environment indoor-outdoor spaces. House Equanimity transmogrifies this typology by utilizing its tenets in a different, even opposite, climactic situation.

From the Southwestern elevation, the living room opens outwards to a double-height deck; the separation between interior and exterior spaces rendered obsolete through axially sliding glass doors. The deck is protected from above by a cantilevered continuation of the house's roof, and selectively shielded from the north via a selectively panelled 'wall'-cum-brise soleil. At the far end of the deck the space simply falls off into its environs. It doesn't so much feel like the structure is ending as it does like it is simply incorporating back into its environment. This serves multiple purposes. While it provides shade and privacy from neighbouring homes, it also functions as a framing device, placing geometric perspective(s) upon the surrounding vistas. In essence, contextualizing itself into its surroundings; making them one.

The upper floor, reached via a floating wooden staircase, contains a master bedroom, which functions as an open 'loft', looking down over the double-height living room, as well as two additional bedrooms and a single bathroom.

The simple, straightforward programme of the house provides a key to the formula of the artist's intended lifestyle, but also a less prosaic reading of his intuitive concept of 'home'. It also, clearly, requires an understanding of the purported occupants. Master bedroom as open loft sans ensuite facilities; two smaller bedrooms, and a single bathroom on the upper floor. One immediately conjures ideas of a family with either small children, or with children who have left for college. A single-family residence typically inhabited only by the maitre and maitresse.

Over the last three decades, the typical footprint of an American single-family house has increased from 1700sq/f to 2600sq/f, as the combination of our in toto succumbing to advertising's espousement of the 'bigger is better' lifestyle trope coalesces with our increased reliance on technological interaction over actual interaction. Alone, together. And, while McMansion design may happily promote FaceTime over face time, familial intimacy is clearly promoted by the sensible sizing and open-plan post-formalism of House Equanimity's floor planning.

Material History

Material drivers come in many forms and motivations. Some geographic or historical, and some philosophical or practical.

Biondo has written in the past about the Shaker philosophy, calling it a 'primary influence' to his work. To wit, 'Don't make something unless it is both necessary and useful; but if it is both necessary and useful, don't hesitate to make it beautiful.' As with all philosophies, it is one of prioritization. The necessary over the aesthetic, to be sure, with an acknowledgement of the aesthetic imperative of design. Simplicity and elegance in the pursuit of functionality. When viewing residential architecture functionality becomes of even greater import, as one's relationship with one's home is paramount. For a home to truly embody its purpose it must feel both comfortable and attractive to its inhabitant, but, above all, functional. Equanimity ably embodies these virtues, creating a work that is palpably practicable, while providing moments of quiet grace and beauty.

Regionality, too, is paramount in architecture; sometimes embodied in a vernacular aesthetic imbued by necessity, sometimes in material-oriented choices made for climactic reasons. Pennsylvania's winters tend towards the caustically harsh, with temperatures oscillating from burning to freezing; and wind, snow, and humidity all inevitably patinating her structures. Indigenous climactic graffiti; plumes of paint marking buildings with the essence of their surroundings as surely as a teenager fumbles with depositing his name on the side of a suburban Seven-Eleven.

Coplay Cement Company Kilns, Lehigh County, Pennsylvania, by Coplay Cement Co. 1893. Photography by Jet Lowe.

Stahl House, Los Angeles, California, USA, by Pierre Koenig, 1959. Photography by Julius Shulman

In casting House Equanimity, Biondo is concerned as much with regional necessity as regional history; the concrete that makes up the house's foundation and structural basis is a rebuke to the area, but also a celebration of it. Northampton, PA is the birthplace of American Portland cement, and the area's landscape is flecked with artifacts of the area's industrial overtures. Disused kilns are permanently embedded in the area, both structurally and metaphorically, and House Equanimity, its primary building materials being site poured concrete and various concrete products, pays respect to this storied past.

Biondo is heavily influenced by the industrial artifacts that are rooted in the Pennsylvanian landscape, having written, 'Today's modern cement plant stands as a strong form consisting of framed boxes perched atop a series of concrete monoliths which loom in the partially monotonous and chaotic surroundings that are suburbia. These industrial machines, along with the material they produce, greatly influence the design of this home'. He has also written at length of a home's need for timelessness in design, and what could be more timeless than concrete. Even the material's homonymic dictionary definitions speak to its timelessness. A building material, sure, but also 'existence in a material or physical forms; real or solid; not abstract'.

Equanimity is founded in site-cast concrete, the sculptural concrete base is topped with site-case concrete that is selectively

manipulated through sand blasting and bush hammering. An amalgam of béton brut and béton brillant, neither brutalist nor specifically modernist, but rather environmental; an ode to the axis of the area's history and material history. As Biondo has said, 'To make an extraordinary material special is trite, but to heighten one's awareness of a humble material can be poetic'.

Regionality

Regionality is and must be a central tenet to residential architecture. In the aforementioned Case Study House programme, one of the central tenets, and central failures of understanding, was its mandate for readily reproducible designs, not taking into account site or regional specificity. Koenig's Stahl House could easily be recreated in a variety of arenas, but stripped of its situation in the Hollywood Hills, with its seemingly never-ending views of the city of Los Angeles, would it be the same? Site and context are oftentimes inextricably linked.

House Equanimity, and Biondo's larger oeuvre, take an enlightened and forceful view of the import of regional awareness. Many of his previous works have been rooted in the decontextualization of the ruins of Pennsylvania's post-industrial decline. His design for the ArtsQuest Centre at Steelstacks, which won an Architizer award for Architecture and Urban Transformation, as well as an AIA PA Silver Medal, pays homage to the area that Walter Gropius once called the 'Mutterland der Industrie'. Cantilevered steel balconies reference the town of Bethelem's eponymous material histories, and the entire complex is seated directly beneath the disused behemoth that is the site's former blast furnaces and smokestacks.

The Ledge House, that he designed in collaboration with Peter Bohlin while working at Bohlin Cywinski Jackson, is an architectural materialization of a specific region's nature in a clarity of tectonic form. As Will Bruder wrote, 'In this work, extremes, edges, and eccentricity combine to form an original, inspired whole. Is is a moment at a clearing in the woods where stone meets log, idea meets reality, invention meets craft, function meets beauty, and the past meets the present. It is a place where the magic of architecture inspires one to relax and dream of what might be!'

House Equanimity continues this philosophical exploration of the recontextualization of regional architectural mores. One in which the ordinary and uninspiring landscape of suburbia need not be a lesser field of lowest common denominator design. Where environment can inspire architecture, rather than lazily inform its basest instincts. As with Koenig's house, Equanimity is raised up by its topography and geography. Reproducible, yes, but inimitable.

The sculptural concrete base of the house is an immediate demonstration of this. The monolith serves as an organizing element, rather than a necessitative afterthought designed to combat the sloping site. Instead, it functions as a figure that can embrace the other layers being organized from within. The stereotomic walls affix themselves into the earth, while lighter tectonic wood-framed, cement panel and glass panels give the feeling

Artsquest Center, Bethlehem, Pennsylvania, USA, by Spillman Farmer Architects, 2010. Photography by Paul Warchol.

Artsquest Center, Bethlehem, Pennsylvania, USA, by Spillman Farmer Architects, 2010. Photography by Paul Warchol.

of emanating from the monolith, rather than opposing it; using it merely for structural support.

House Equanimity occupies a particular place in Biondo's heart, as it was originally built for himself and his family. It was conceived as a personal statement, and not simply one of design. He has written at length of his conception of this house as a site-specific installation; something as much 'of' as 'on' this particular patch of land. He refers to its foundation as a 'planted concrete ruin', one that is inextricably linked to its location, and its material choices as ones that invite the natural erosion that Pennsylvania's climate all but guarantees. Like a living thing, it will age and slowly erode; with the intangible dimension of time slowly leaving her marks. A rolling stone may gather no moss, but a static one surely does.

Nature of Architecture

Architecture is unique amongst creative métiers. Rather than being simply an aesthetic or conceptual expression, meted out in trochaic metres or swaths of paint, architecture exists on a precarious razor's edge between art and science; expression and engineering. Painting, poetry, and cinema are wondrous forms of communication, but, by their very nature, experiential aspects

must be intrinsic; emotive. We interact with them abstractly, spiritually, even narcissistically (in the Lacanian sense), but not tangibly. With architecture, however, those interactions are broader; simultaneously more elaborate and more focussed. Because while we can experience architecture from an extrinsic perspective, as with a traditional artwork, we also interact with it from an intensely personal place, intrinsic by its very nature. Interactions aren't peripheral, they're environmental, and practical needs must be observed. On the other hand, architecture imbues our very lives; a well designed home quite literally has the power to make every day better; brighter; more productive.

As Entenza later went on to write:

'What man has learned about himself...will, we are sure, express itself in the way in which he will want to be housed in the future. Only one thing will stop the realization of that wish and that is the tenacity with which man clings to old forms because he does not yet understand the new.

It becomes the obligation of all those who serve and profit through man's wish to live well, to take the mysteries and the black magic out of the hard facts that go into the building of "house".'

Ledge House, Catocin Mountains, Maryland, USA, by Bohlin Cywinski Jackson, 1996. Photography by Karl A. Backus.

Ledge House, Catocin Mountains, Maryland, USA, by Bohlin Cywinski Jackson, 1996. Photography by Karl A. Backus.

DESIGN

PREFACE
BY JOSEPH BIONDO

BELIEFS ON MAKING A HOME

We are living in a period increasingly enamored with high technology. The world keeps moving faster and faster. Therefore it is not unreasonable to believe that people regard their private domain as a safeguard against an inhospitable world of uncontrollable change. Linked to our primitive need for shelter, the house has been a symbol of status, personal freedom and individuality for centuries. Owning a private single-family home remains the dream for most individuals today. Throughout the country, sprawling new developments present us with the ideal dream home much like an automobile dealership introduces us to its latest models. All somehow alike, there is little evidence of professional input on design and they are too often placed upon the landscape without imagination and consideration for the ecological consequences of increased sprawl.

"Exquisite building lots available - choose your model from our set of stock plans." These are familiar words from a billboard perched upon the pristine landscapes and farmland of Pennsylvania—evidence that production housing is on its way. From its post-war inception, production housing was created to provide the "American dream" in an efficient, economical, and predictable manner through means of standard building procedures and well-known imagery. Since then, our housing has been increasingly reduced to profit-driven, known merchandise that builders can build, bankers can finance, and real estate agents can sell. In producing these houses, ease of construction and time are paramount (time of construction that is—not time that records the history of a building or forecasts its uses). Landscapes are stripped of trees and vegeta-

tion and significant topographical characteristics, are flattened. Ecosystems are abruptly altered so lot owners can express their individuality. In an attempt to create a tranquil world of familiar situations, we have been left with peculiar landscapes and soulless containers or bad copies of historic archetypes that are adapted to meet our excessive lifestyles. They are an attempt to fulfill the perceived immediate needs for the traditional nuclear family, but do little to meet the many possible demands of future generations.

Beyond site consideration, programmatic needs of a client and issues of sustainability, thoughtful planning of a house must include its ability to produce a lasting or timeless aesthetic. By employing time-honored materials that respond organically to the process of nature, an overall fabric whose appearance is improved with the weathering of time is achieved. In addition, carefully planned details that enhance structural integrity can also influence the appearance and form of a home. The choice of materials, quality of construction and the technical resolution of its parts endow a home with a character beyond that of an exaggerated expressions or short-lived fashion statement. Herewith presented is a home developed from a tectonic language and focus on the process of production rather than the product itself. A house whose floor plan is influenced by the topography it nestles within. Through the directness and unadorned exposure of the manner in which it is made, it attempts to do more than demonstrate some narrow architectural issue. It represents architecture that is clear, precise, honest, and reflects on what is absolutely necessary. An architecture whose form is developed from the intense working of materials and their means of construction—an exploitation of materials and connections whose sensory and tactile qualities are revealed and further heightened through the movement of light. Here is a building which does not depart from the latest technologies nor substitute them for the fundamental components of a building. The choice to use certain materials in this house is driven by an aesthetic, functional requirement and largely reflects ties to regional traditions.

My curiosity with materials of modest means is explored in all of my architecture. By using ordinary materials we gain the greatest possibility of achieving a renewed reality within the material condition of a building. The materials I prefer to use are commonplace however, the care for their methods of assembly and absolute passion for scrupulous detailing are not. It is the detail which becomes the means for heightening and transfiguring the mundane, raising curiosity and elevating the human spirit. To make an extraordinary material special is trite, but to heighten one's awareness of a humble material can be poetic. Concrete and concrete has been relegated to areas of a building hidden below grade or behind finished walls, possess unique qualities. Concrete, a fluid material that takes the shape of its form, is a product that is very versatile in its use, workability, and surface treatment. Nothing can be more elemental, humbler in substance, modest in manufacture, and simpler in shape and texture. More than any other building systems, concrete can be married to many other materials whether natural or man-made: wood, metal, glass, cementitious panels.

Through rigorous and precise application of these complimentary materials, the status of concrete, which is so simple and so ordinary, can be elevated. Each material has particular characteristics, which, through careful and appropriate treatment, a distinct expression can develop.

House Equanimity is constructed using site-cast concrete that is accepted as is, and then, much like a fine stone, is further manicured by sand blasting and selectively bush hammering of its surfaces. In detailing this house, nothing is to be taken for granted. Whether it be exploiting the module of a material, the detail of a stair riser meeting a tread, or the layout of the whole. An orthogonal plan or an intentionally austere, barrier-like, street façade seem deceptively simple from outward appearances. Upon closer investigation, the interiors seem to radiate a sense of tranquility through their appropriate scale, materiality, and detailing. The physical line between exterior and interior is now masked through the continuity of a particular material. Interior zones are brought into accord with zones of materials. A journey through the home becomes a series of discoveries that are developed through to the smallest detail.

DESCRIPTION

Situated in a typical nondescript subdivision of Eastern Pennsylvania, this home is surrounded by other single-family houses of all shapes and sizes, redolent with clichés and conventions which can be just as easily elsewhere as here. For that reason it is the surrounding landscape and history of the region that largely determines the design. The primary building materials, site poured concrete and various concrete products, pay respect to the history of Northampton – the birthplace of American Portland Cement.

Permanently embedded into the landscape of Northampton and now standing proudly in ruin, are the industrial artifacts which record the history of cement making. Kilns which were used to melt the rock quarried here, developed over time. The initial Dome kilns were inefficient and gave way to the Schoefer kilns which could operate continuously. Within a decade, the Schoefer kilns were replaced with rotary kilns whose technology remains in existence. Today's modern cement plant stands as a strong form consisting of framed boxes perched atop a series of concrete monoliths which loom in the partially monotonous and chaotic surroundings that are suburbia. These industrial machines, along with the material they produce, greatly influence the design of this home.

The house is not a solitary cube that might have been sited anywhere, but one which penetrates into the landscape and becomes one with it. This single-family, three bedroom home deviates in scale and appearance from the neighboring houses. In fact it seems closer in spirit to the forest and topography it nestles within. The main living area, whose face is half buried into the landscape, offers no views to the east except that of its walled courtyard. It is to be a peaceful place, a kind of oasis sheltered from sound and views of the subdivision thus creating an outdoor room that opens to the sky. The interior space is open, intimate, and neutral with domestic objects articulated as furnishings placed within.

The base of the home is constructed of concrete. This seemingly unnatural mixture of fluid stone and steel reinforcement is quite sufficiently different fro historical materials. However, it is a material that offers the rough, tactile charm that often emanate from the irregularities of mature buildings. Deliberately crude in its execution, the concrete monolith is treated as an existing condition, or ruin, whose subsequent wood-framed, cementitious clad boxes are carefully inserted. The ruin's powerful presence is derived from its material qualities and from the way it is linked to the ground. It penetrates into the earth and engages a platform which becomes clearly defined as the topography falls away.

The planted concrete ruin looks as though it is going to be in the location it has found for itself for a long time. Unlike its surrounding production housing counterparts, it is not even thinking of moving away from the place it occupies and defines by its very existence. The concrete is allowed to age, become rough and perhaps slowly erode. The intangible dimension of time could then be recorded by the traces left on the walls. Eventually, gravel will be exposed and particles of dirt, algae, and moss will take hold.

This home is an architecture that involves all the senses. The surfaces and details demand to be felt. The spaces and special sequences require to be grasped by the senses that apprehend gravity, driving forces, and temperature. Details involving human contact such as entrance areas, steps, handles and hand rails are treated with particular care. The restricted tolerances of construction elegantly contrasts with the random nature of the organic while the massing, textures, and unevenness of weathering surfaces transmit similar sensations to the landscape.

SKETCHES

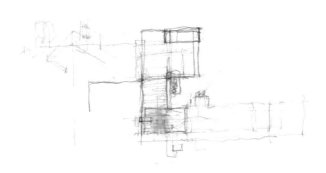

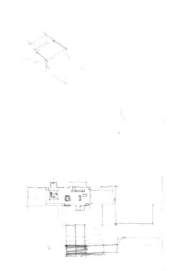

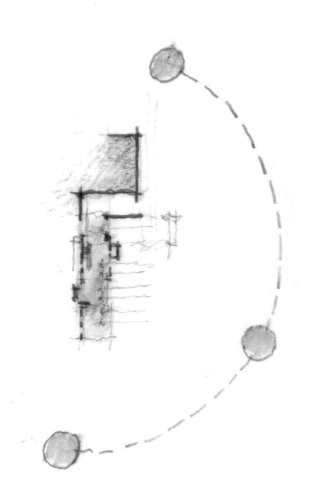

HOUSE PARTI

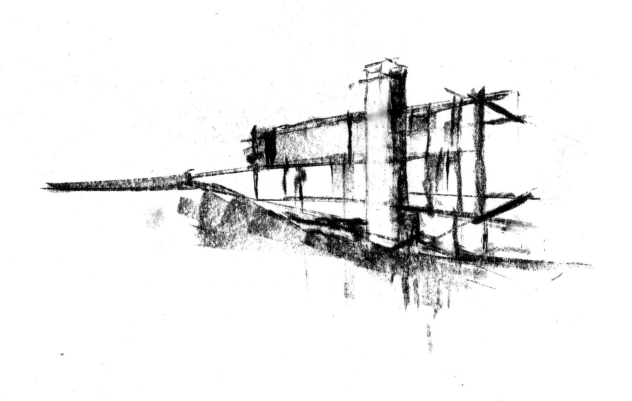

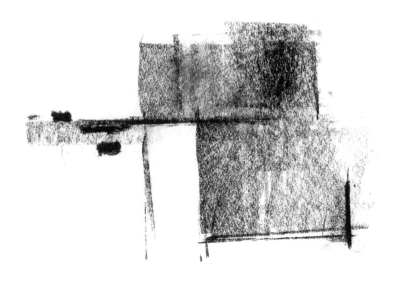

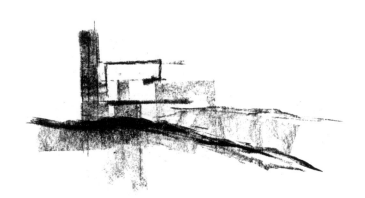

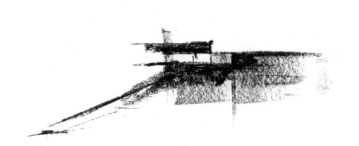

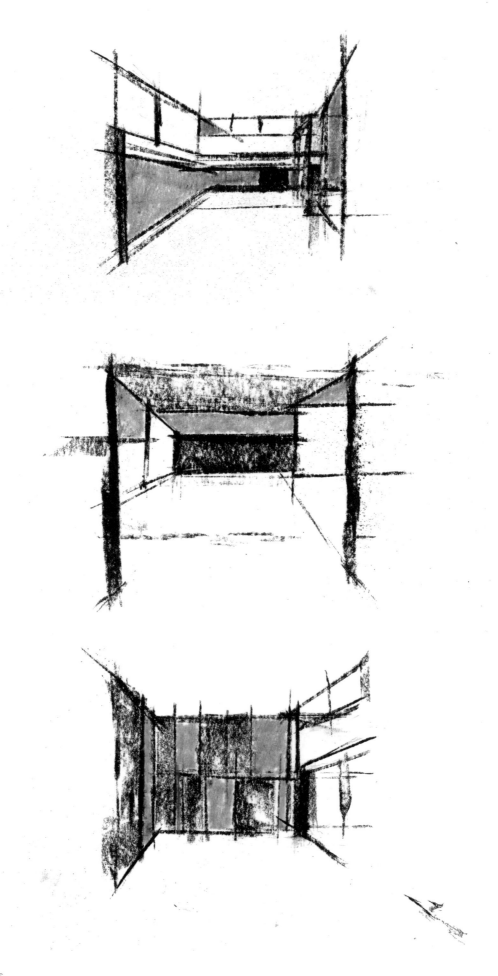

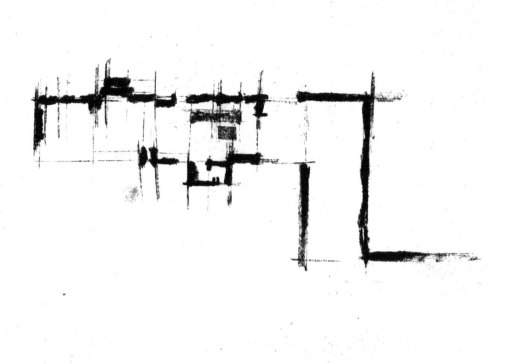

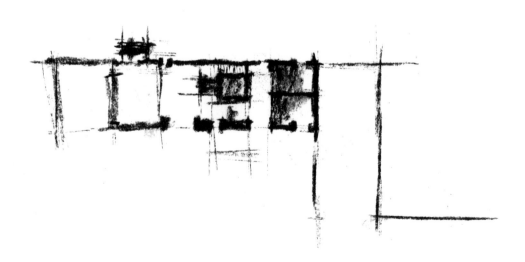

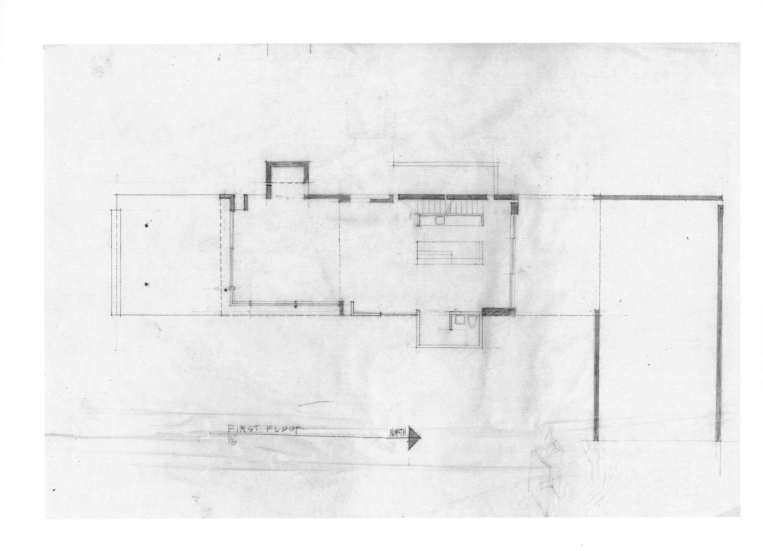

FIRST FLOOR
⅛

NORTH ▶

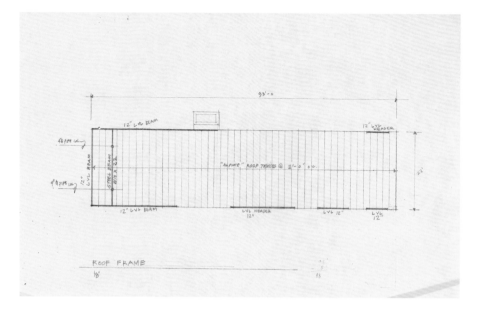

ROOF FRAME
1/8"

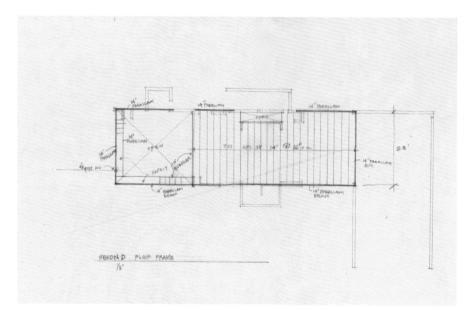

SECOND FLOOR FRAME
1/8"

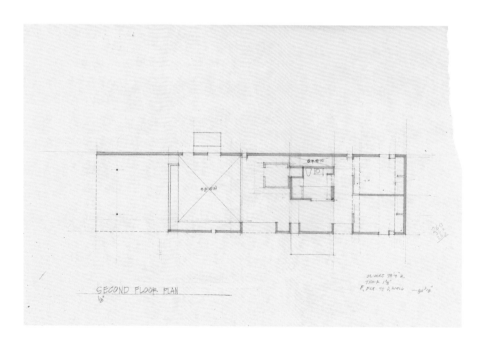

SECOND FLOOR PLAN
1/8"

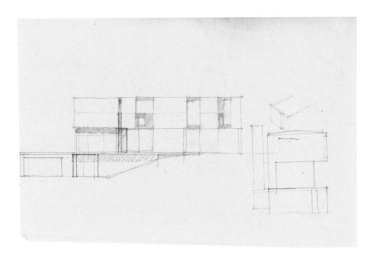
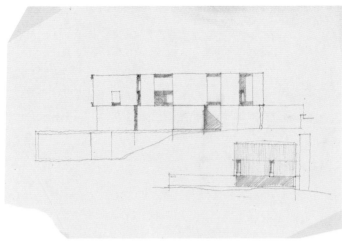
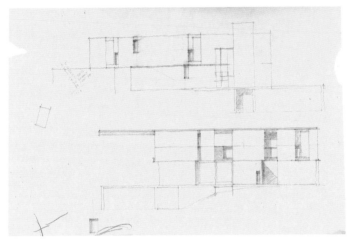
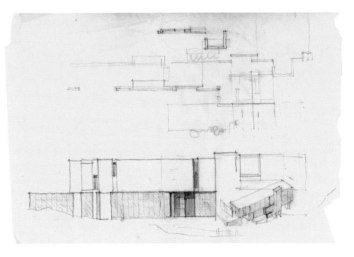

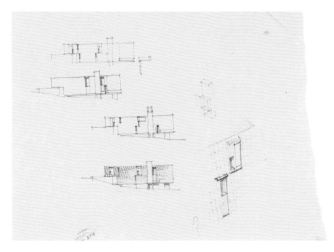

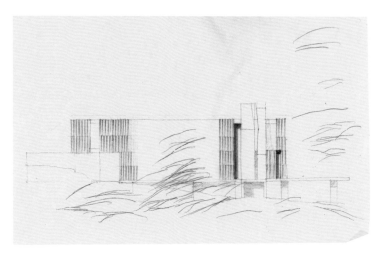

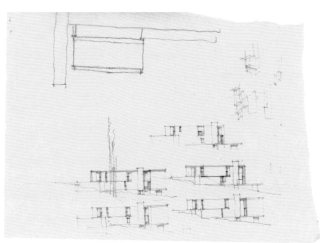

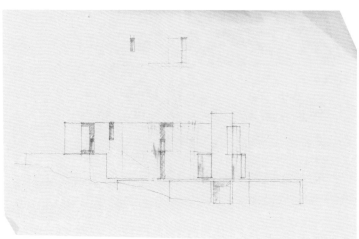

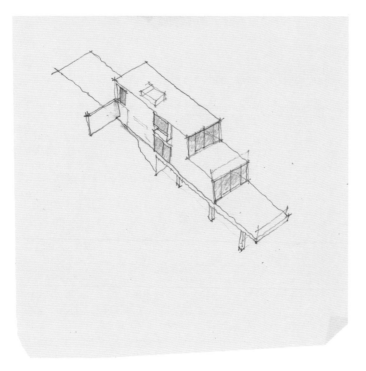

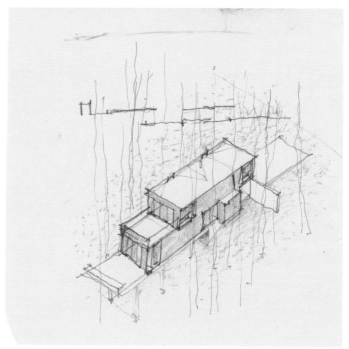

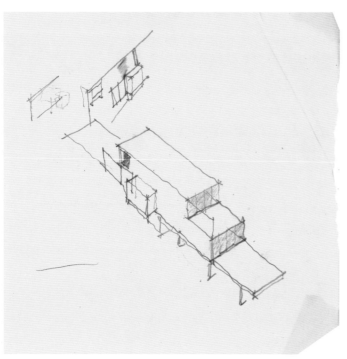

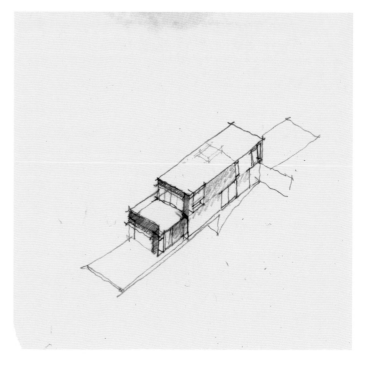

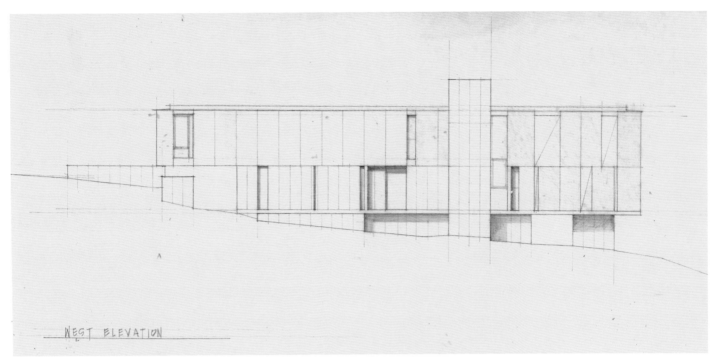

WEST ELEVATION

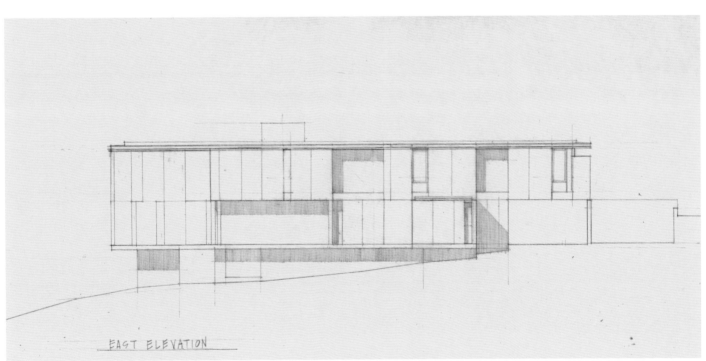

EAST ELEVATION

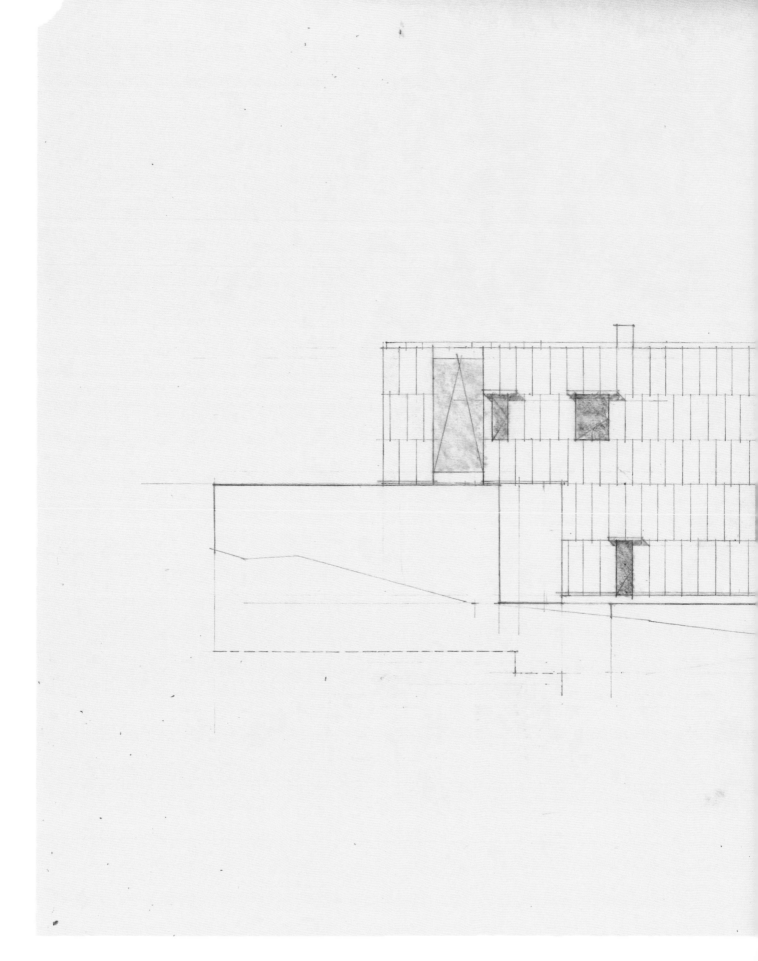

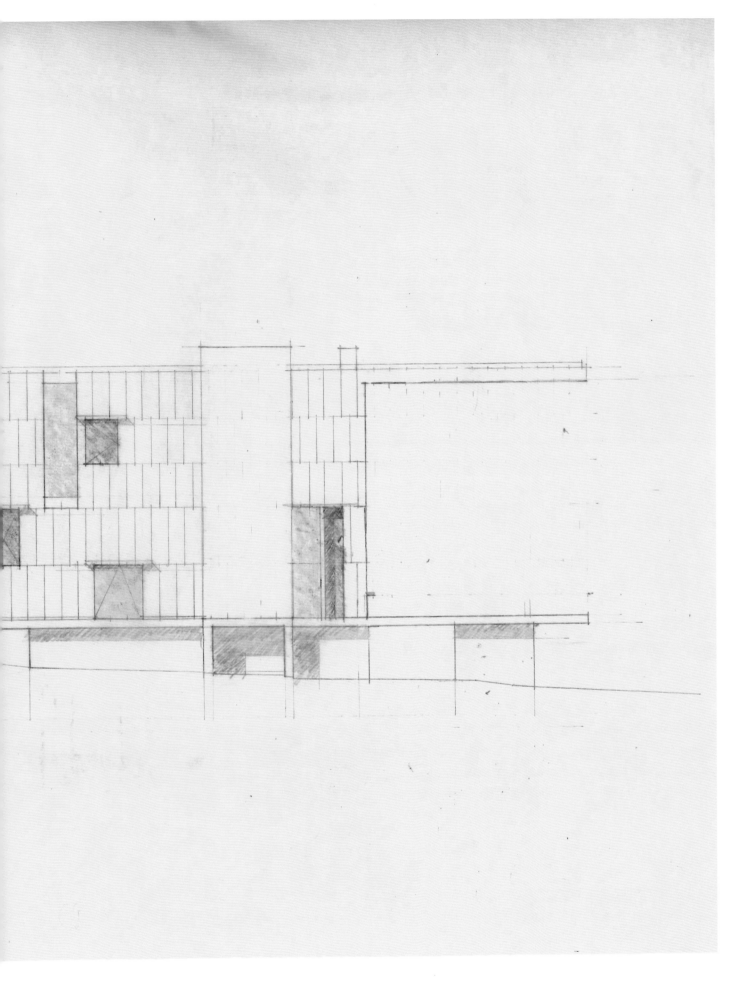

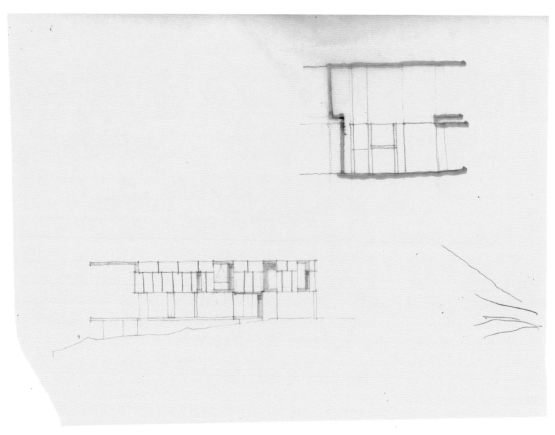

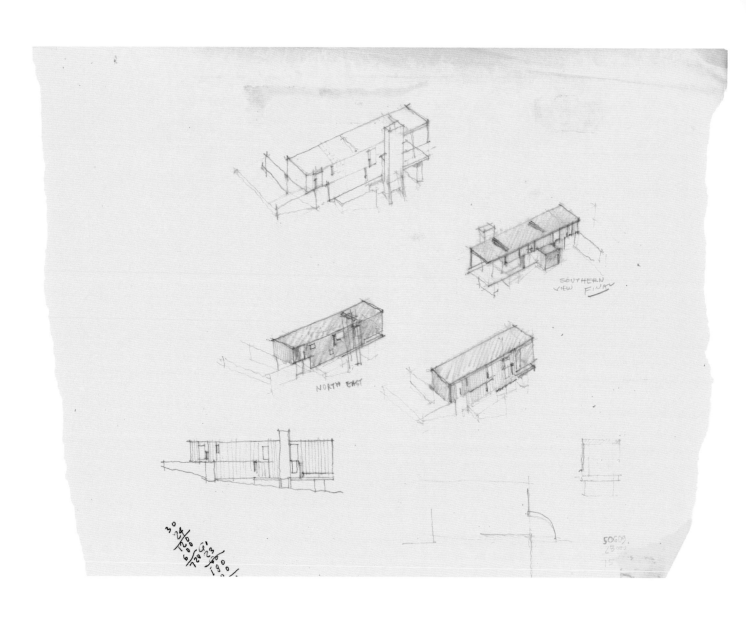

SOUTHERN
VIEW FINAL

NORTH EAST

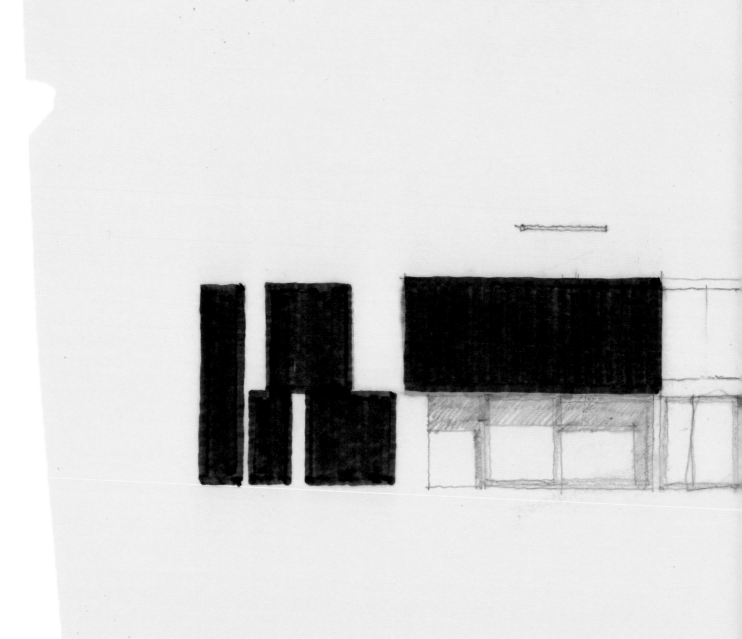

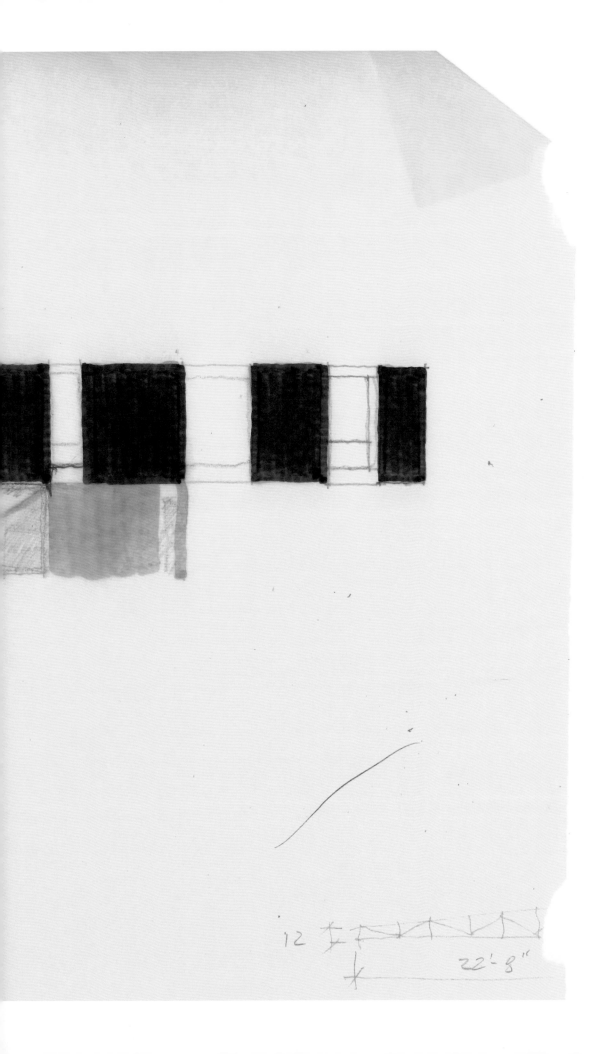

12 22'-8"

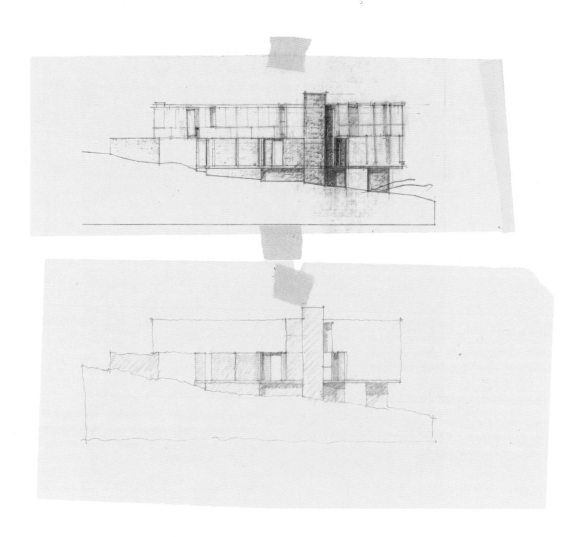

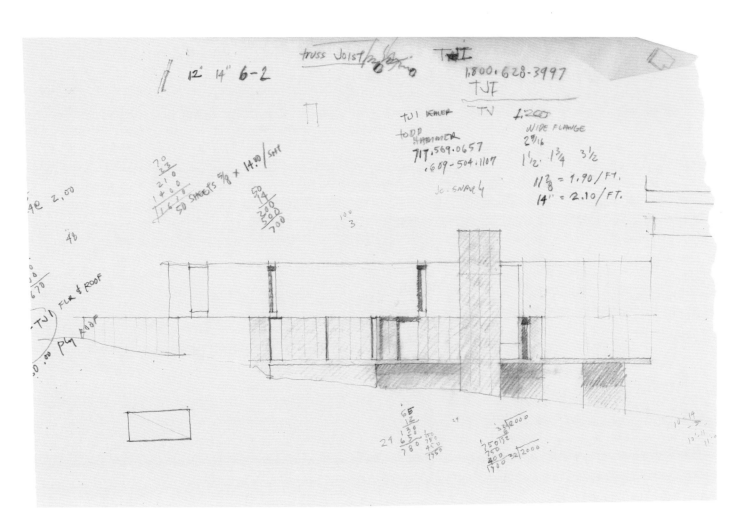

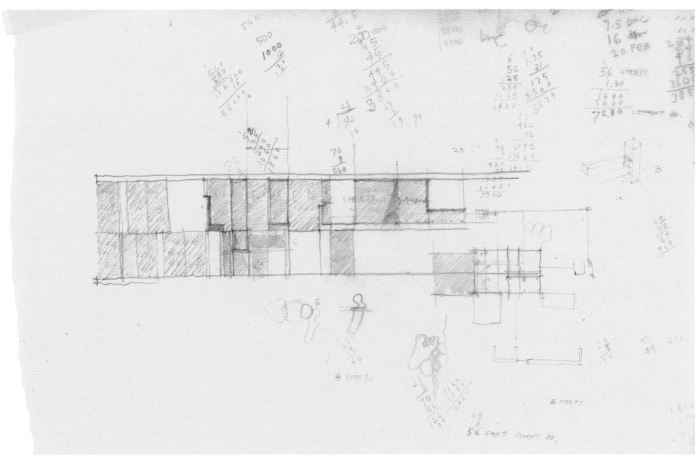

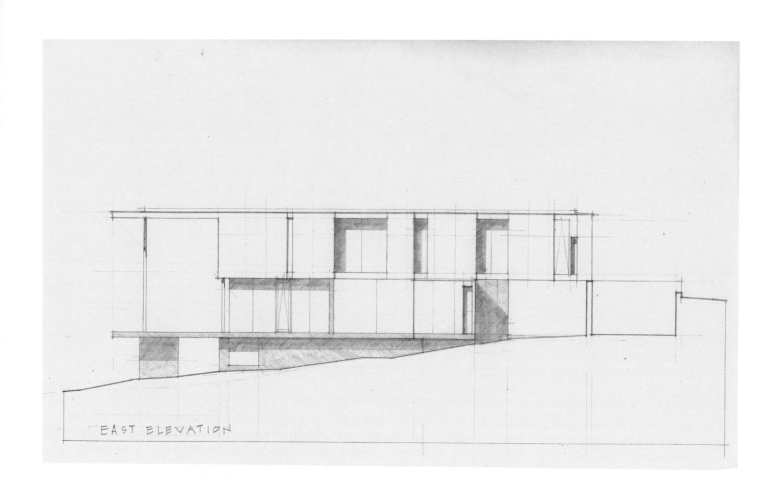

EAST ELEVATION

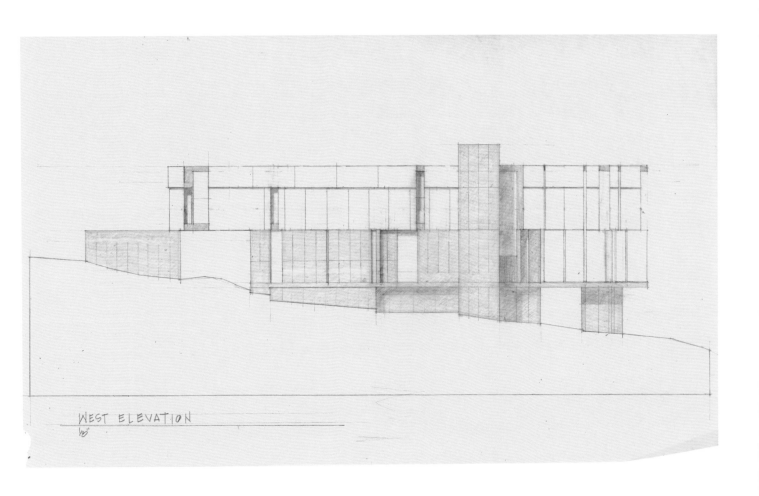

WEST ELEVATION

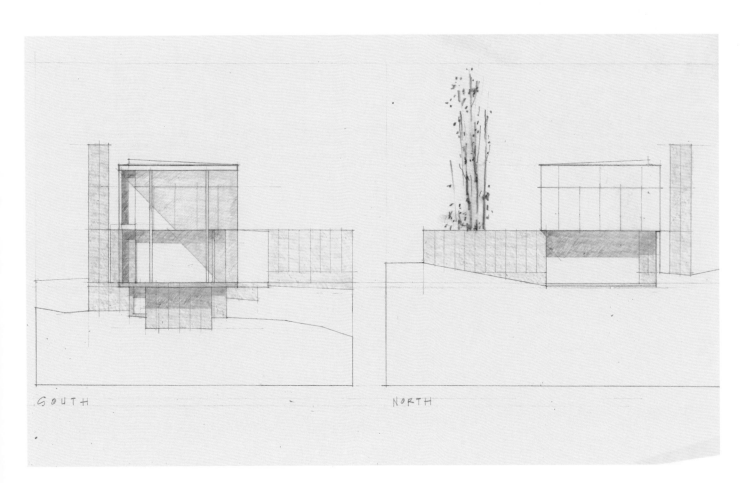

SOUTH   NORTH

section

PRESENTATION DRAWINGS

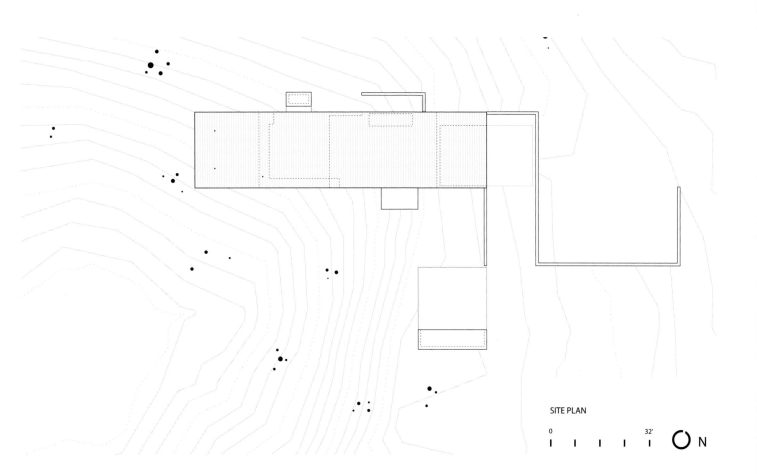

SITE PLAN

0   32'

N

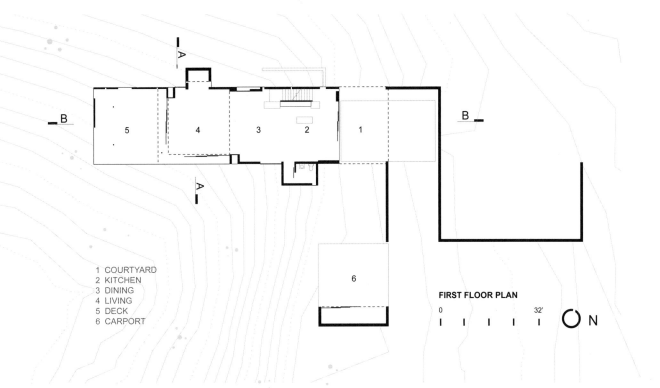

1 COURTYARD
2 KITCHEN
3 DINING
4 LIVING
5 DECK
6 CARPORT

FIRST FLOOR PLAN

0   32'

N

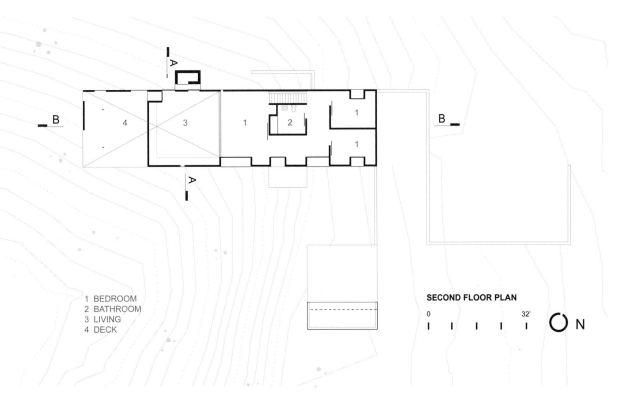

1 BEDROOM
2 BATHROOM
3 LIVING
4 DECK

SECOND FLOOR PLAN

0   32'

N

1. Courtyard
2. Kitchen
3. Dining
4. Living
5. Deck
6. Bedroom
7. Bathroom
8. Basement

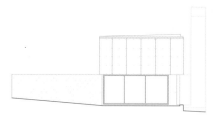

East Elevation

0   20'

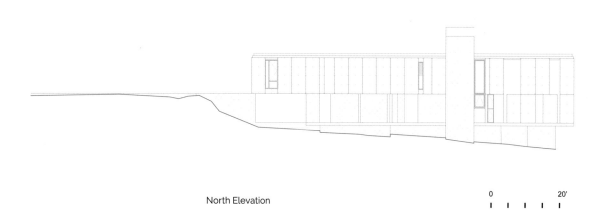

North Elevation

0   20'

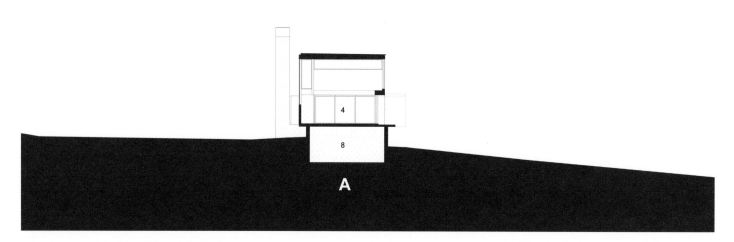

4

8

A

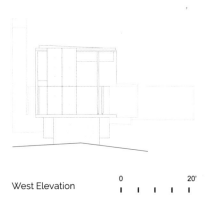

West Elevation

0   20'

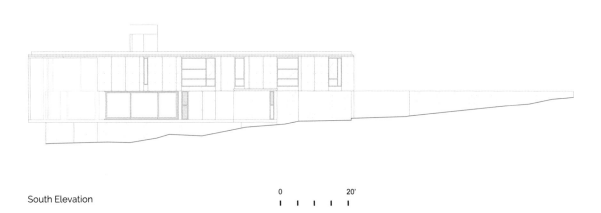

South Elevation

0   20'

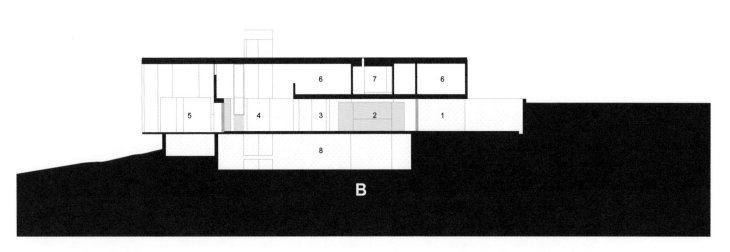

| 5 | 4 | 3 | 2 | 1 | 6 | 7 | 6 |
| 8 |

B

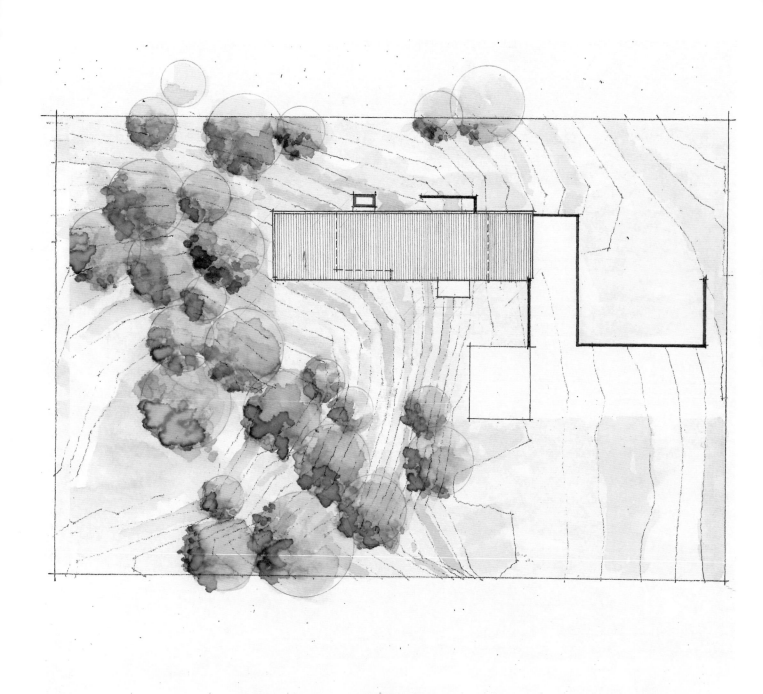

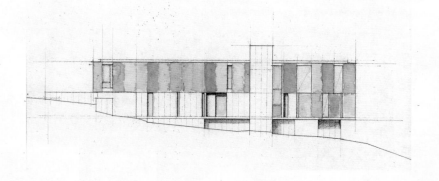

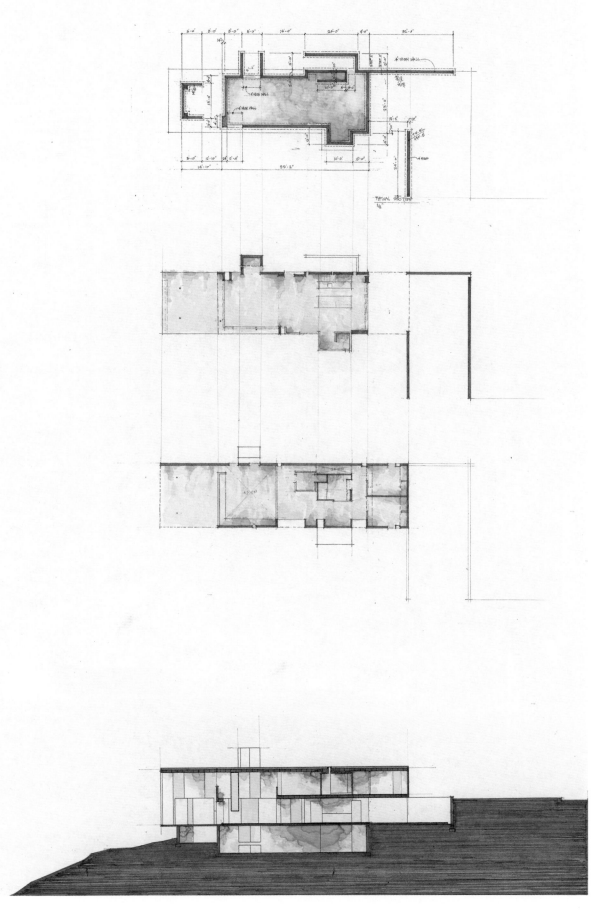

MODEL VIEWS

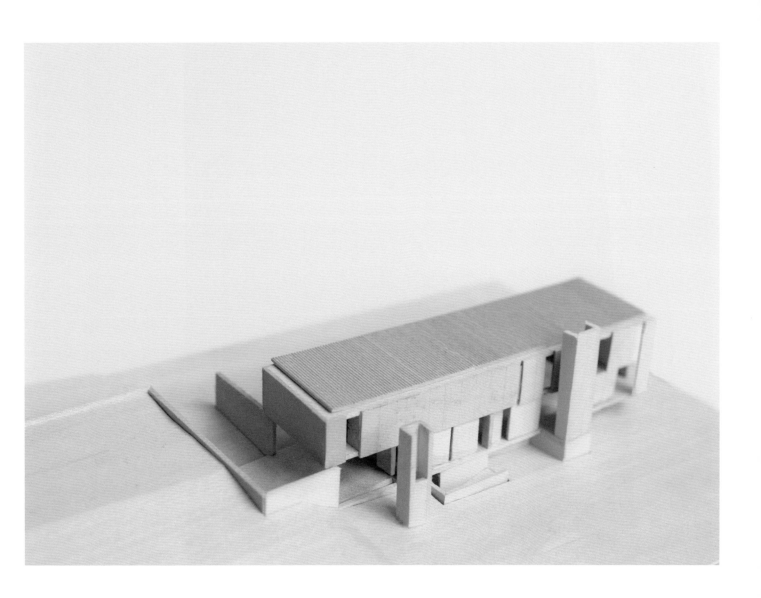

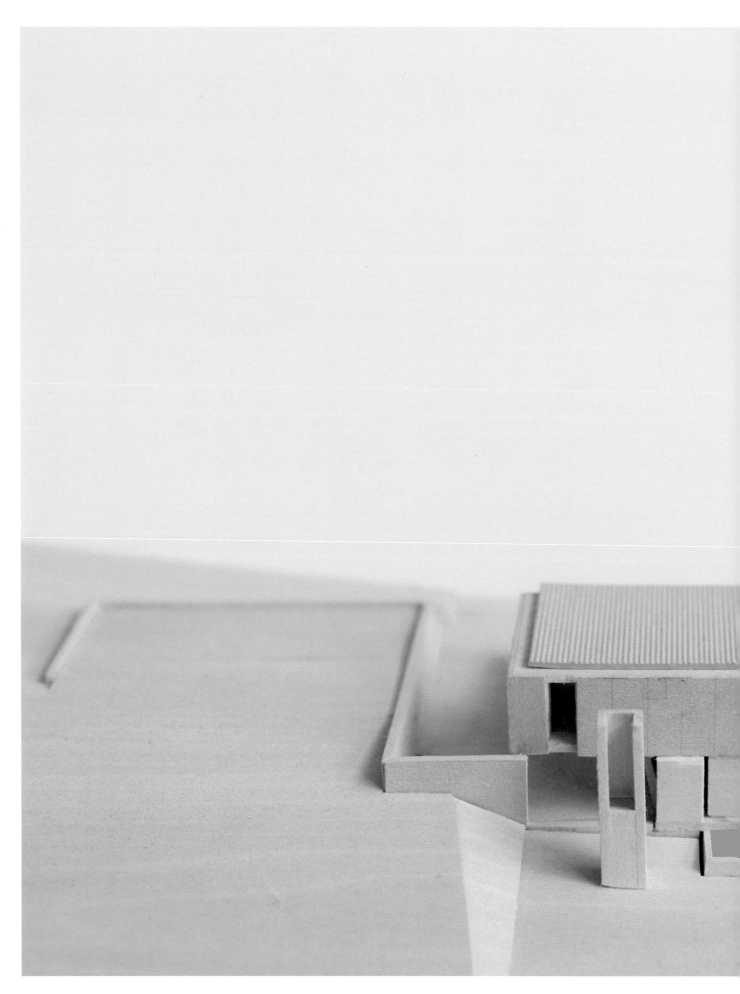

CONSTRUCTION

WORKING DRAWINGS

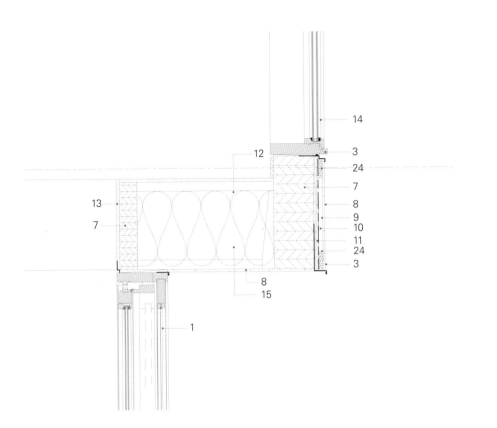

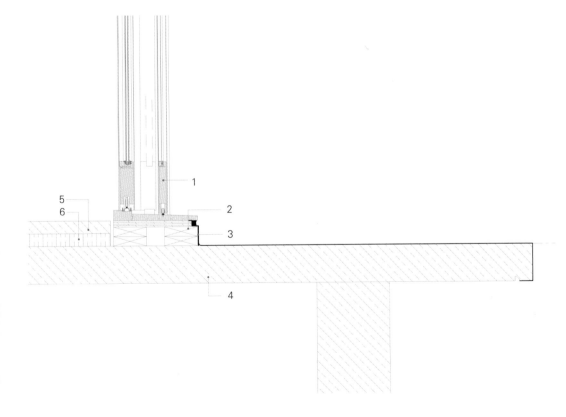

1. Wood sliding glass system
2. Wood blocking
3. Lead coated copper flashing
4. 8" Reinforced structural concrete
5. 2" Sealed concrete topping
6. 2" Rigid insulation
7. Engineered timber beam
8. 7/16" Cement board
9. 3/4" Wood furring & air space
10. Air & vapor barrier
11. 5/8" Plywood
12. Batt thermal insulation
13. 5/8" Gypsum wall board
14. Wood fixed window
15. 14" TJI floor joist
16. 12" TJI roof joist
17. Waterproof membrane
18. 7/8" Corregated metal roof
19. 3/8" Veneer plywood (stained)
20. 2x6 Wood stud framing
21. Exposed reinforced concrete wall
22. Wood roof joist
23. Wood casement window
24. Insect fabric
25. Flat lock lead coated copper sheet metal
26. Neoprene flute infil

Detail at sliding glass wall

0   1'

1. Wood sliding glass system
2. Wood blocking
3. Lead coated copper flashing
4. 8" Reinforced structural concrete
5. 2" Sealed concrete topping
6. 2" Rigid insulation
7. Engineered timber beam
8. 7/16" Cement board
9. 3/4" Wood furring & air space
10. Air & vapor barrier
11. 5/8" Plywood
12. Batt thermal insulation
13. 5/8" Gypsum wall board
14. Wood fixed window
15. 14" TJI floor joist
16. 12" TJI roof joist
17. Waterproof membrane
18. 7/8" Corregated metal roof
19. 3/8" Veneer plywood (stained)
20. 2x6 Wood stud framing
21. Exposed reinforced concrete wall
22. Wood roof joist
23. Wood casement window
24. Insect Fabric
25. Flat lock lead coated copper sheet metal
26. Neoprene flute infil

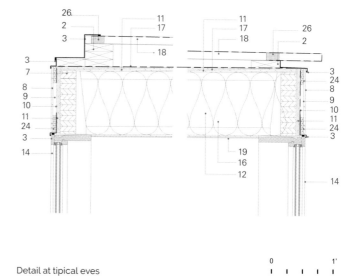

Detail at tipical eves

0   1'

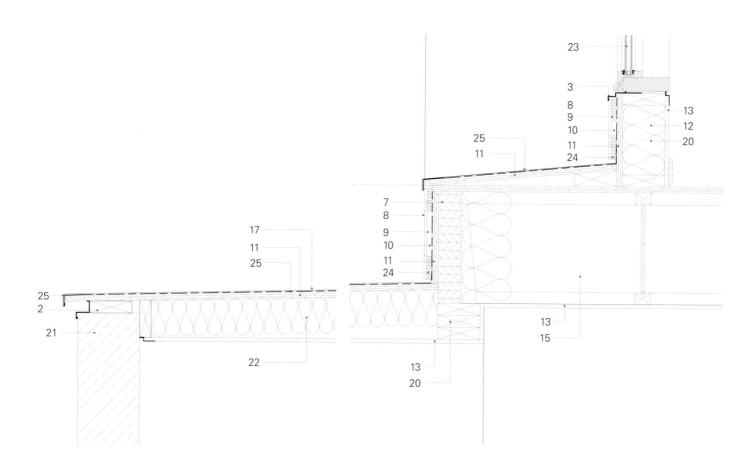

Detail at low roof and deep sill

0   1'

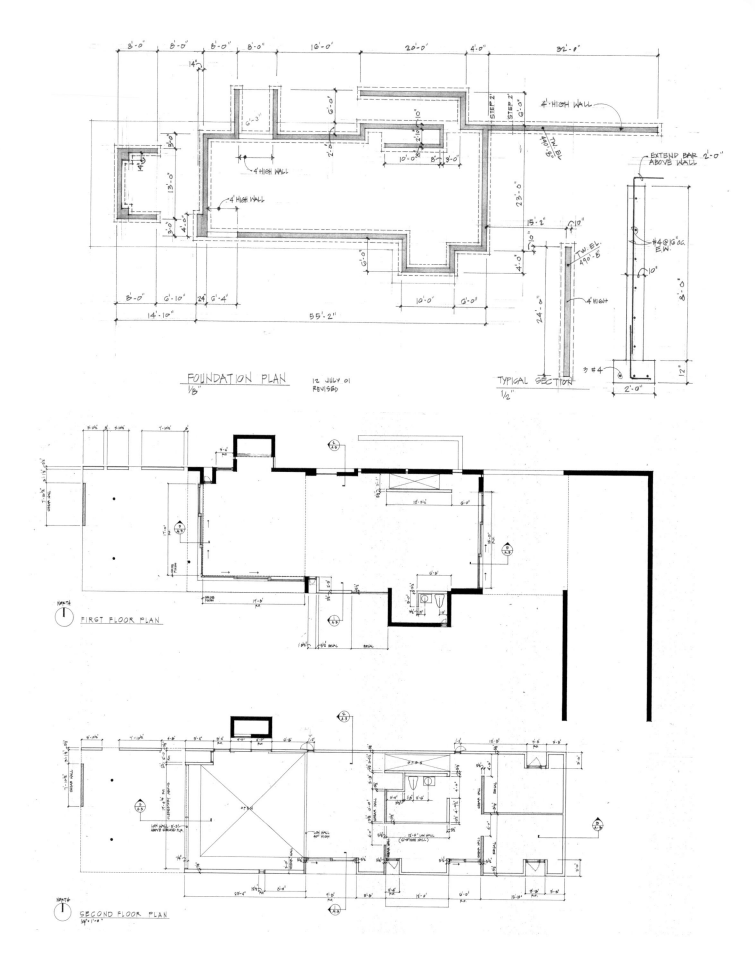

FOUNDATION PLAN
1/8"

12 JULY 01
REVISED

TYPICAL SECTION
1/2"

FIRST FLOOR PLAN

NORTH

SECOND FLOOR PLAN
1/4"=1'-0"

NORTH

NOTE:
TOP OF WALL EL. 490'-00
UNLESS NOTED

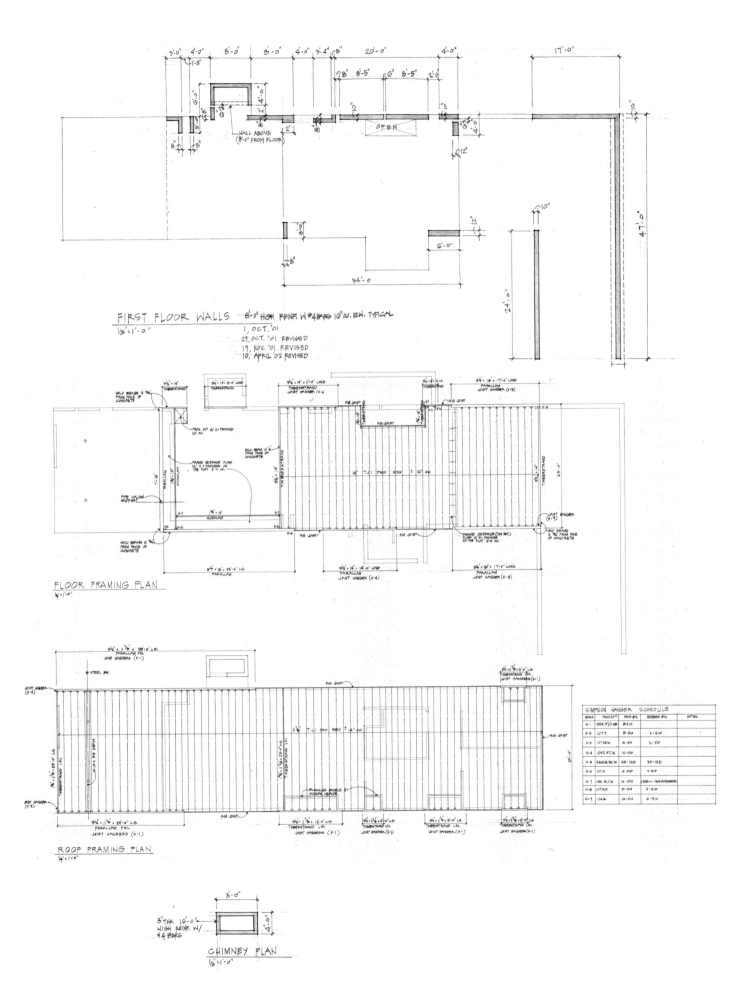

FIRST FLOOR WALLS — 8'-0" HIGH REINF. W/ #4 BARS 10" O.C. E.W. TYPICAL
1/8" = 1'-0"

1, OCT. '01
29, OCT. '01 REVISED
19, NOV. '01 REVISED
10, APRIL '02 REVISED

WALL ABOVE
(8'-0" FROM FLOOR)

OPEN

FLOOR FRAMING PLAN
1/4" = 1'-0"

ROOF FRAMING PLAN
1/4" = 1'-0"

CHIMNEY PLAN
1/8" = 1'-0"

8" THK. 16'-0"
HIGH REINF. W/
#4 BARS

SIMPSON HANGER SCHEDULE				
MARK	PRODUCT	FACE NAIL	MEMBER NAIL	NOTES
H-1	1206.3/1.88	8-N10		
H-2	IUT9	8-N10	2-N10	
H-3	IUT3814	14-N10	2-N10	
H-4	IU62.37/14	12-N10		
H-5	HGUS.38/14	88-16D	22-16D	
H-6	IU14	4-N10	2-N10	
H-7	1281.81/14	12-10D	40B+1-14B x THROUGH NAIL	
H-8	IUT410	8-N10	2-N10	
H-9	18416	10-N10	6-N10	

077

PROCESS

THE BUILDING

EPILOGUE

BY JOSEPH N. BIONDO

A platonic form emerging with the landscape

Ours was a very unique and gratifying experience. As Owner, Architect and Contractor, we were challenged with opportunity of balancing building's concept, construction cost and material craft. Decisions had to be carefully considered and presaged the emergence of a slow architecture - where architectural components were built over time, each becoming one with the site in the process of its construction; existing conditions were continually revisited.

The sculptural concrete base is an example of this. The monolith becomes an organizing element with sufficient size, closure, and regularity to serve as a figure that can embrace the other layers being organized from within. The heavy stereotomic walls affix themselves into the earth while the lighter tectonic wood-framed, cement panel and glass envelope appears to hover above grade. As a planted ruin, it may begin to tell the story of how and why it was made. The image during construction (2003) may be similar to that in 5003. The flanking reinforced concrete walls provide sufficient structure and enclosure which enable the main living area to be free of interior walls. The absence of these walls offers uninterrupted connectivity to the landscape.

With consideration to the Virtruvian theory of *Utilitas*, *Fermitas* and *Venustas*, the focus is on the first two; utility and structure. There is a complete focus to execute those fundamentals of program and structure extraordinarily well and in doing so, the attractiveness is achieved.

We have made a place for memories - a very comfortable home which can also be considered as an intriguing construct that challenges the ordinary and uninspired landscape of suburbia.

APPENDIX

BIOGRAPHY

Joseph N. Biondo, FAIA was born in Bethlehem, Pennsylvania and graduated from the Kansas State University. Shortly after graduation, he pursued a lengthy career with the firm of Bohlin Cywinski Jackson Architects where he worked closely with AIA Gold Medal recipient Peter Bohlin. In 1996 he established JOSEPH N. BIONDO ARCHITECTS before joining SPILLMAN FARMER ARCHITECTS in 2003 where he is currently bringing design excellence to the forefront. Joseph Biondo's architecture is recognized for its ties to regional traditions. His buildings represent an architecture that is clear, precise and honest and reflects on what is absolutely necessary. He specializes in an architecture whose form is developed from the intense working of materials and their means of construction-an exploitation of materials and connections whose sensory and tactile qualities are revealed and further heightened through the passage of time.

His work has been recognized by his peers in the American Institute of Architects (AIA) and has been featured in the profession's most prestigious publications. Joe's work celebrates the "process of making" and is deeply influenced by his family background, which is rooted in the garment and construction industries. Biondo's core belief is that beyond site considerations, client program requirements, and issues of sustainability, thoughtful planning of a building must include its ability to produce a lasting aesthetic. By employing time-honored materials that respond organically to the process of nature, an overall fabric whose appearance is improved with the weathering of time is achieved. In addition, carefully planned details that enhance structural integrity will also influence appearance and form of a building. The choice of materials, quality of construction, and the technical resolution of its parts endow a building of a character beyond that of an exaggerated expression or short-lived fashion statement.

PROJECT CREDITS

Architect
Joseph N. Biondo

Location
Northampton, Pennsylvania, USA

Client
Biondo Family; Jospeh, Catherine,
Michael and Abrienne

Project
2009

Completion
2010

Area
2600 square feet

Budget
Budget witheld at owners' request

Collaborators
Joseph Balsamo
Randy Galiotto
Siera Krause
William Miller
Dan Silberman

Interior Design
Joseph N. Biondo

Structure
E.D Pons Associates

Contractor
Hoffert General Contractors
James J. Christman Electric
Grube Plumbing and Heating

Photography
Steve Wolfe
Joseph N. Biondo (construction photos)
Dan Silberman (model photos, aerial
photos)

CONSTRUCTION

Structural System
Reinforced concrete, engineered
lumber and structural steel

Exterior Cladding
Concrete:
Reinforced cast in place concrete
Wood:
Weyerhaeuser trus joist
James Hardie cement panels

Roofing
Metal:
McElroy corrugated galvalume
Other:
Lead coated copper flashings and
sheet metal

Windows
Wood:
Duratherm

Doors
Entrances:
Duratherm
Sliding doors:
Duratherm

Hardware
Locksets:
Gretsch-Unitas Hardware

Interior Finishes
Cabinetwork and custom woodwork:
Jonathan Fallos Cabinet Makers
Paints and stains:
SIKKENS, Sherwin Williams

Lighting
Interior ambient lighting:
Lightolier
Downlights:
Lightolier

Plumbing
Toto
Duravit

Electricity, Heating and Cooling
Hot Water heating; Wirsbo radiant
floors, Runtal radiators, Weil-Mclane
Boiler

Electrical Systems
400 amp service

Plumbing System
Weil-Mclane boiler. copper hard piping.
Wirsbo PEX radiant floor

Plumbing Fixtures
Vola, Hansgrohe, Grohe

Bathroom Fixtures
Duravit

Kitchen Installation
Jonathan Fallos Cabinet Makers

PHOTOGRAPHY CAPTIONS

View from street depicting living spaces half buried in the landscape.

Detail of East façade with glimpse of interior. Cementitious clad wood box perched over concrete monolith.

South view.

Exterior detail of mass/void rhythm and materiality.

Construction process. Foundation, early stages.

Construction process. The excavation and forming of concrete footings. Preparing for the pour.

Construction process. The pouring of concrete foundations and retaining walls.

Construction process. The pouring of concrete foundations and retaining walls.

Construction process. Forming of reinforced concrete foundation and preparing for the pour.

Construction process. The backfill with concrete foundation in place.

Construction process. Joe Biondo with son Michael observing construction of footings.

Construction process. Embed into the landscape, the reinforced concrete foundation walls in place, waterproofed and backfilled.

Construction process. The reinforced concrete foundation walls in place preparing to backfill.

Construction process. The reinforced concrete foundation walls in place, waterproofed and backfilled.

Construction process. The reinforced concrete foundation walls in place, waterproofed and backfilled.

Construction process. Concrete platform preparation. Joe Biondo tying reinforcing bars.

Construction process.
The first floor forming of the
reinforced concrete platform.

Construction process.
The first floor forming of the
reinforced concrete platform.

Construction process.
The first floor reinforced
concrete platform.

Construction process.
The first floor forming of the
reinforced concrete platform.

Construction process.
The first floor reinforced
concrete platform.

Construction process.
The first floor forming of the
reinforced concrete platform.

Construction process.
Forming site retaining walls.
Releasing forms from the first
floor concrete walls.

Construction process.
Releasing forms from the
first floor concrete walls.

Construction process.
Releasing forms from the
first floor concrete walls.

Construction process.
Concrete monolith rising from
the site and taking form.

Construction process.
Fireplace mass.

Construction process.
Concrete monolith rising from
the site and taking form.

Construction process.
Embed into landscape, the
concrete monolith rising from
the site and taking form.

Construction process.
Extending out over the site, the
wood framed boxes are perched
above concrete monolith.

Construction process.
Extending out over the site, the
wood framed boxes are perched
above concrete monolith.

Construction process.
Extending out over the site, the
wood framed boxes are perched
above concrete monolith.

Construction process.
View from Northeast; an austere yet rhythmic façade punctuated by the fireplace mass.

Construction process.
View from Southeast; living spaces emerge out of the site. The wood framed boxes perched above concrete monolith.

Construction process.
View from Southeast; living spaces emerge out of the site. The wood framed boxes perched above concrete monolith. Mass/void proportions taking shape.

East façade winter shot of last construction stages.

Winter shot during last construction stages.

Winter shot during last construction stages.

Southeast winter shot of last construction stages.

Construction process.
View from Southeast; living spaces emerge out of the site. The wood framed boxes perched above concrete monolith.

Construction process.
View from Southeast; cementitious clad sleeping spaces perched above concrete monolith.

Construction process.
View from rear porch into living spaces. The layers of concrete monolith are evident.

Construction process.
View from street depicting living spaces half buried in the landscape.

Construction process.
Double height living room preparing for paint.

Construction process.
Double height living room preparing for paint.

Construction process.
Double height living room preparing for paint.

Aerial view from Northeast.

Aerial view from Southeast.

Aerial view from East.

Mailbox detail.

Mailbox detail.

Mailbox detail.

Mailbox detail.

Mailbox detail.

Le Corbusier stenciled adress in mailbox.

View from Southeast; living spaces emerge out of the site. The cementitious clad, wood framed boxes perched above concrete monolith.

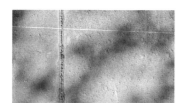

Concrete cube projection, platform living spaces open to landscape.

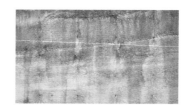

South facade details; material, composition, textures, shadows.

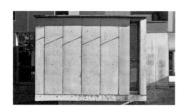

Shadows on concrete.

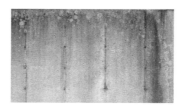

Concrete detail.

Concrete and window detail at powder room.

Aged concrete. Accepted "as-is" and unadorned.

South Elevation.

Extending out over the site, the living spaces open up to the landscape.

Northwest Elevation.

Rhythmic cut outs of cementitious façade enclosing rear porch.

Interior of rear porch. Rhythmic cut outs of cementitious façade provide privacy while enclosing rear porch.

North Elevation.

Natural markings of concrete from black walnuts.

Exterior detail.

Bearing detail on concrete monolith.

North facade growing out of the landscape.

View from Northeast; an austere yet rhythmic façade punctuated by the fireplace mass.

Approach to entry porch with living spaces beyond.

View out to entry court from living space.

Terrace detail.

Detail of East façade with glimpse of interior. Cementitious clad wood box perched over concrete monolith.

Exterior at dusk.

Exterior detail.

Interior/exterior at dusk.

Dusk view of south elevation. Living and sleeping spaces view out to landscape.

Double height living space extends to rear porch and landscape beyond.

The primary living space extends to the outdoors and opens up to the double height porch.

Living room.

Detail of wood shutters and windows placed within the concrete walls.

Coat hooks; accessories drilled into concrete.

Winter exterior view from living room.

Interior detailing.

Interior bench detail.

Kitchen - domestic objects are articulated as furniture placed within the concrete and glass envelope.

Mercer Tiles.
"Architecture builds the house".

Mercer Tiles.
"Literature teaches the house".

Mercer Tiles.
"Music gladdens the house".

Mercer Tiles.
"Art decorates the house".

Kitchen sink detail.

Staircase landing.

Floor and wall details.

Wall detail.

Floor, wall, and stair detail.

Wood stairs are a series of floating platforms which slip by the hand hammered concrete wall.

Morning sunlight through stairs grazing textured concrete wall.

Detail of towel bar and wood shutter placed within concrete wall. Radiant concrete floor floats from walls.

Detail of wood shutter placed within concrete wall. Ceiling edges appear to float from concrete surfaces.

Living room from master bedroom.

Master bedroom.

Bathroom.

Winter view.

Winter view.

Winter view.

Winter view.

South Elevation.

Interior of rear porch. Rhythmic cut outs of cementitious façade provide privacy while enclosing rear porch.

BOOK CREDITS

Book Editing and Layout by Oscar Riera Ojeda

OSCAR RIERA OJEDA
PUBLISHERS

Copyright © 2018 by Oscar Riera Ojeda Publishers Limited
ISBN 978-1-946226-06-8
Published by Oscar Riera Ojeda Publishers Limited
Printed in the USA by Brillant Graphics

Oscar Riera Ojeda Publishers Limited
Unit 4-6, 7/F.,
Far East Consortium Building,
121 Des Voeux Road Central, Hong Kong

Production Offices | China
Suit 19, Shenyun Road,
Nanshan District, Shenzhen 518055
T:+86-135-5479-2350

www.oropublishers.com | www.oscarrieraojeda.com
oscar@oscarrieraojeda.com